T0115041

Baby Boomer Ramblings

Reflections on Life through Childlike Eyes

Gene McParland

BALBOA.
PRESS
A DIVISION OF HAY HOUSE

Copyright © 2014 Gene McParland.

All rights reserved. No part of this book may be used or reproduced by any means, graphic, electronic, or mechanical, including photocopying, recording, taping or by any information storage retrieval system without the written permission of the publisher except in the case of brief quotations embodied in critical articles and reviews.

Balboa Press books may be ordered through booksellers or by contacting:

Balboa Press
A Division of Hay House
1663 Liberty Drive
Bloomington, IN 47403
www.balboapress.com
1 (877) 407-4847

Because of the dynamic nature of the Internet, any web addresses or links contained in this book may have changed since publication and may no longer be valid. The views expressed in this work are solely those of the author and do not necessarily reflect the views of the publisher, and the publisher hereby disclaims any responsibility for them.

The author of this book does not dispense medical advice or prescribe the use of any technique as a form of treatment for physical, emotional, or medical problems without the advice of a physician, either directly or indirectly. The intent of the author is only to offer information of a general nature to help you in your quest for emotional and spiritual well-being. In the event you use any of the information in this book for yourself, which is your constitutional right, the author and the publisher assume no responsibility for your actions.

Any people depicted in stock imagery provided by Thinkstock are models, and such images are being used for illustrative purposes only.
Certain stock imagery © Thinkstock.

Printed in the United States of America.

ISBN: 978-1-4525-9424-8 (sc)
ISBN: 978-1-4525-9426-2 (hc)
ISBN: 978-1-4525-9425-5 (e)

Library of Congress Control Number: 2014904398

Balboa Press rev. date: 04/03/2014

Dedication

This book is dedicated to the poet in all of us, and
to those who can see life through the eyes of a child.
Life is a journey - have fun along the way!

Contents

Introduction

What a gift life is. It comes ready to open every morning. Each day is unique. Every 24 hours is a new adventure. It can be a source of joy, or of sorrow. It all depends on how we approach it. Learn to look at life through the eyes of a small child and it's an adventure. Look at life through glasses of self-pity and want, then life is a struggle filled with unsatisfied desires. I've lived life both ways and I know which way I prefer to live now.

I'm a bona fide baby boomer. I've lived life filled with many joys and many regrets. Today I choose living life in joy with a sense of childlike wonderment. Believe me I remember my regrets, often much more than I should. Today I try looking at them as some of life's lessons. Many of these lessons could have been learnt a lot quicker than they were, but my thick Irish head sometimes likes banging against the wall of life way longer than it needs to.

This then is one of the reasons for writing this book. It's a collection of my ramblings and experiences about, dare I say it, the meaning of life. Herein I offer my thoughts, observations, and suggestions on living life in a more positive and happier way. Hey, there's some good advice here! At the minimum these selections offer some food for thought on how to live in the moment. How to live life with a sense of awe and childlike glee. How to live life a little off-centered, being a little out of step with society's dictated norms. And all of this wrapped around a poem, or more correctly, a poem wrapped around life's gifts.

Personally, I prefer to live life as a poem. We poets tend to do things like that. Musicians use music. Artists use paint and other mediums. Poets paint with words. We sing our songs of life with poetry. Everything I do can relate to a poem (yes, even that!).

Poetry adds magic to life. It's the mind's and heart's way of expressing one's inner voice. Unlike a text book on life which is read, poetry is recited by one's mind and speaks to one's heart and spirit. It is a very unique way of expressing thoughts and feelings in a few words instead of writing paragraphs and pages of text.

We are all poets even if we don't know it. I know, I know, a bad rhyme, but that's OK. It says what it means to say. We all have the voice of a poet, a musician, an artist inside of us. It's part of our creative soul. It is what connects us with the god-force. When we become creators, we transcend the mere human aspects of our being. When you really get down to it, it makes us more human in the good sense of the word.

Poetry is to be savored. You don't speed read poetry. If you do, you end up missing the whole point of the piece. Poetry like life is not meant to be rushed. You miss all the richness of it, if you do - you miss those nuances that make life a beautiful experience.

Poems are not narrative. They don't follow the same rules as a story or novel. They go off on tangents and often stay there. A poem wants to speak to you. The language of a poem is often condensed. Reread one if it seems to confuse you. Poetry is meant to be read aloud; try it. This way your senses are more open to the poem's message. Expect to find surprises. They are there.

As a baby boomer I've experienced around two-thirds or so of my life by now. At this stage I'm finally getting it - what's really important in order to find and experience happiness. Unless I really screw up I'll probably make it into my senior years. I want to be one of those elders that you meet that have that special glint of childhood mischief and adventure in their eyes. I want a life of fulfillment, not one of false wants and regrets. I want a life filled with contentment and laughter. A life where the glass is always at least half-filled because I'm drinking out of it and not worrying that it will become empty. I am not interested in living a life where I see the glass as half-empty; a life of constant want and worry.

Half-Full

I seem to be in a ½ full kind of way.
Rain in the morning,
sun in the afternoon,
sun in the morning,
rain in the afternoon.
My life seems ½ over;
or is it only ½ begun?
I don't know.
Things just feel kind of ½ way to me.

½ full, ½ empty,
my mood chooses.
Good mood – ½ full;
Bad mood – ½ empty;
Really down mood – ½ empty and in a dirty glass.

Well, right now I seem to be in a ½ full way,
½ way through the day.
Even my poem seems to go only ½ way
to the point
that I wish I knew that I was making.

Oh well,
some days are just like that.

When tomorrow comes,
I'll give it my full attention.
But not today.
Heck, it's ½ over anyway.

Approaching Life with Childlike Wonderment

There is only one way to see our world, and that is through the eyes of a child. It seems that only children can be one with the wonderment of the NOW. Whether it be the secret world of the lawn; the magic of a tidal pool; the dance of swaying trees, a cloud ballet in the sky, a child can see what we adults often miss. They know about God. They talk with him. She talks with them.

Sure bills are important, but in the final analysis what will have more impact on your life? Knowing that you paid your electrical bill on time or that flowers are magical designs of color, and some are homes to fairies? What has more impact on your life - reading and knowing what is in the newspaper front to back, or laying in the grass next to a small child and observing a whole universe of life and exploration right there before your eyes?

Who are the happiest old people that you know? Those who categorize each complaint of their body, or those who see life through the eyes of a child? Those who try to control every situation and the lives of others, or those who love and accept the childlike wonderment in all of us? Those who hold on to every feeling, or those who release them and move on? Those who bitch constantly about their yesterdays, could-have-beens, should-have-beens, or those who live and love their todays?

Life is life. It isn't what we might consider "fair"; it just "is". We can approach our circumstances in many different ways. The choice is ours. It always has been. It is the "adult" within each of us that judges and accepts/rejects the circumstances around each of us and chooses how to react.

I tend to view life through the eyes of a poet and a child. To my eyes there is a flowing to all that I perceive going on around me. I can pick and choose those aspects of life that I want to involve myself with. I can open to all that flows to me, and follow where my heart and spirit takes me. A child's spirit naturally follows a path that leads to joy and fulfillment, which should be the natural inclination of one's true spirit.

The wind blows; the rain falls; a spirit accepts what is happening and goes with it. A poet uses such situations as manna for creating and expressing. A child knows that the wind is a needed ingredient for flying kites. A child will follow leaves blowing in the wind; watch birds soar and glide in it. An adult will complain that all the leaves seem to be landing on his lawn.

Rain can monetarily ruin a sunny day; sidetrack plans for going outside. The child might be saddened by the rain at first, but will open up to new adventures within the house - an adventure in the basement among old toys; a fantasy created with toy figures on a crumbled blanket. A rainy day can be an invitation to create with crayons, markers and such. Let rainy days become your invitation to become that childlike artist again. Let it allow you to become that poet of nature. Always be open to rainy day adventures, if only in your mind.

I might be older in body these days but not in spirit. I advise all to be open to the worlds of fantasy and exploration. A child can easily become bored, but will not stay in that state long if he/she can help it. An adult can easily become bored, and will often remain stuck in that state. Often you have to light a fire under someone's bottom to get them moving again. You may need to do it to yourself. Be alert!

The bottom line is to never become bored of spirit. Open up - create - explore - become that child with eyes of wonder - be that poet of life!

Childhood Clouds

I hope that I never lose
my childlike nature.
When clouds cease to be
a source of wonderment;
newts and frogs
creatures of magical appeal.

When dragons no longer
protect secret lairs;
when I no longer want to lie
(or is it lay?)
in the grass
watching bees and ants;
I know that my soul

will cease to grow.

I vote that alarm clocks get banned,
TV News goes unwatched.
I hope that dandelions remain
the bouquet of choice for little children.
That I will always want
to eat peanut butter off the knife,
and suck nectar from the ends
of yellow honeysuckles.

The world of the child
is amazed by falling leaves
in the breeze;
clouds in the sky.

You know this is
still true for me.

Escape to Nature to Heal

When the "stuff" of life gets to be too much and the proverbial fecal matter hits the proverbial fan, then it's time to escape back into Nature. It is not so much an "escape" as a "return" to Nature.

Nature has a way of soothing our pains. The female nurturing aspects of Mother Gaia have long been a natural pressure release valve for all. Its calming effect is often just the right medicine to help an ego-controlled mind put things into their proper perspective. Because when you size-up your problems surrounded by a forest of trees or looking out over the vastness of an ocean its real insignificance often becomes quite apparent.

If you have no ocean or forest conveniently nearby, then just tilt back your head and look up into the vastness of the sky. An ocean of air and clouds or a tapestry of stars at night can easily work its magic on your soul. Their beauty and serenity can easily help you through difficult emotions.

We humans are not separate from our earth. When you stop and quietly become attuned to your senses, you realize that Mother Gaia is a nurturing entity far beyond our realm of comprehension. There is even a branch of science that explores this reality. Nature urges one to think of existence and life beyond our usual concepts and beliefs of what we believe "life" is. If one but stops and considers the total inter-relationship of our lives and the environment we would quickly realize that this planet is a giant unified organism existing within the vastness of the universe.

The poet in us has always understood this concept. Obviously not the scientific realities, but when one views life from the heart and spirit one knows - one just knows.

Having trouble in your life? Just go into Nature. Quiet the mind. Listen - open up - absorb - connect. You will quickly feel the poetry of existence; hear its music; find the peace you search for. Nature will more than sooth you; it will awe you.

Cathedral of the Trees

In the depths of the woods
within the cathedral of the trees,
listening to the hymns of life,
I stand in silent adoration.

Tree branches rise toward the heavens,
arms of the supplicants
moving in the breeze;
an African church congregation
swaying to the gospel music of glory.
A choir of birds and insects
join voices in a Gregorian chant
of love and praise.

No stained glass windows
needed to sanctify the light;
the light of grace
bathes me.

Praying from my soul
not for gold or fortune,
but offering prayers
of love and thanksgiving
for the present moment joy
that I am part of
in communion with the One.

And in the silence,
silhouetted by the setting sun,
I say vespers.

A sudden parting of the living canopy;
I am engulfed in brilliant radiance;
a transubstantiation of my spirit
into the god light.

I am completely at peace.
The cathedral resonates
with my hymn of love.

Death is Not the End

The greatest poem on death that I have ever read is John Donne's "Death Be Not Proud". A close runner-up would be "Ode to an Athlete Dying Young" by A. E. Houseman. John Donne's poem sums up the whole impact on death right there in the title - death be not proud. Ode to an athlete dying young, while painful, leaves us with the message that our memory will be carried forth as we were in life. How do most people picture John F. Kennedy? As a youthful smiling president, or as a man who would be in his 90s today?

Death is part of the human process. In Western society we seem to mostly speak of it in hushed terms, while on the TV in the next room life is being terminated at almost every change of the channel. Just watch the evening news; it is one of the most depressing sources of anxiety known to man.

We try not to think about death too much. Most of us prefer to keep it in some locked closet in our minds. It is our constant traveling companion, and it will certainly be there at our final destination stop, almost like it is waiting to collect us at the baggage claim area of life. So as it is so often said, you better learn to enjoy the trip, because whether you like it or not we all end up at the same destination in the end.

Life is meant to be lived in the present moment, or it should be, if you really want to enjoy it. Real living is spontaneous without limits of time. Yes, death is out there, but it should not be in all our present moment experiences. It's just a by-product of living. Whether one lives a full life or one filled with anxiety and fear, the end result is the same. Death is always there just down the road apiece - we just don't usually know how far down the road. Live a happy life; live a sad one. Death waits. It is very patient. We usually are not.

There's a lot of poetry out there about living and enjoying the simple pleasures of our present moments. There are a lot of sad poems and sad songs out there, too. Which do you prefer -reading or singing? Each of us has the choice at any moment to choose which pathway of feeling to walk on.

I have suffered many losses in life, and there certainly will be more. In this I am not alone. It is in our sharing of these feelings and experiences that we shape our humanism and our life.

On some level we all realize that we are only temporary travelers here. We're not too crazy about this fact, and we do our best most of the time to ignore it, or suppress it, which is basically just being human, I guess. Spending our days thinking about death is not a productive way to live life. It is not present moment living. It is not stopping-and-smelling-the-roses thinking. Realizing that we are temporary should give us pause to do exactly that - stop and smell the roses.

What a waste of existence it is to tiptoe through life being too afraid to experience it. As it is often said, we live the length of our lives but not the width of it. Life is a participatory activity. It is meant to be lived in present moment segments.

Small children can do this. We can too. Our poetry of life should honor the beauty we see and experience. Our poems should be more than a collection of melancholic odes to death.

If life teaches us anything, it's that it is meant for the living, not the waiting. Life is an "ing" experience, not an "ed" one. We might need to process the data and events of our daily lives but that is not our goal. Our goal: live in the totality of our existence. Learn to live the poetry of your own life. Death will appreciate hearing these poems on your final journey.

Death is not an ending. It is a transition. The spirit in us continues on its eternal journey after the ego is laid to rest. Our poetry of life lives on!

Sermones ad Mortuos

Here is a sermon to the dead;
to the dead of the flesh,
not of the spirit.
Believe this:
there is life eternal.

Look at the flowers,
the new buds on the trees.
Forget any anguish in your heart.
It is only the death cry of ego.

Let the dragons consume the flesh.
Offer your heart in sacrifice
on the altar
of the all-supreme Self.

Turn to the universe
and feel the Light.
Let the soul be reborn again into Love.
The flesh is temporal;
the soul eternal.

Open to love and forgive.
For in forgiving thou shalt receive.
The spirit shall never die.
This sermon,
not in praise of death,
but of life everlasting.

Beach Glass and the Concept of Timelessness

The weather today was wonderful; wonderful for mid-fall. A very sunny day; it was more spring-like than late fall - a kind of day not to remain indoors and work on the computer, or any other of that indoorish kind of stuff. So I got in the car did a few errands; then magically my vehicle headed toward the beach - Robert Moses State Park on Fire Island, and I wasn't the only one there that's for sure.

You know, the sound of the ocean is very magical. It can't be captured by any recording system no matter how sophisticated or expensive. No recording system can duplicate the richness and timbre that being there at the real shoreline gives you.

Listen to the ocean, it will put your system back in synch. I find it so soothing - it quiets the continual ego bedlam that goes on upstairs somewhere behind the eyeballs. It helps put things back in perspective. The colors of the sky become much more magical as they mix out there on the horizon where ocean and sky meet.

I love walking the shoreline, watching the waves wash up and recede. Waves never end at the same spot; they dance and play along an imaginary line somehow drawn in the sand by the Infinite. I love watching the birds soar and dive. I love the freshness of the smells.

I'm something of a beachcomber. You never exactly know what will be deposited on the shore by the waves. I look for beach glass. Someone asked me recently "what is beach glass", and this is not the first time that I've been asked this question. I just thought everyone knew what it was. I guess I was mistaken for the second time in my life (joke intended). Anyway, beach glass are those pieces of glass, mostly from broken up bottles, that have been tossed about by the ocean and finely sanded by the sands of time until they have rounded edges and a satin finish. Anyway, I've collected jars of beach glass over the years.

I sometimes compare beach glass to us ("us" being baby boomer-aged people). Why? Because we start off so fresh with a shiny finish. We are filled to the brim with the essence of ourselves. Over the years we often become drained by life; discarded; broken up; and lost in the ocean of life. But are we really lost? Or is the essence of us really just released to the universe? Ahhh! Now there's the real question that needs to be answered, and the one that I find so intriguing.

My feeling is this. Positive people feel that they are released by this journey of life. People with lost hope feel drained and discarded like broken pieces of glass at the curbside.

Anyway, I find true beauty and uniqueness in each piece of glass, and I treasure them all. Look for the beauty in yourself and others. The journey of life has made you more treasured, and truly unique.

Beach Glass

Sometimes, I believe, we are like the beach glass
I collect along the shoreline.
Once we were like new,
shining, highly polished;
containing the essence of who we are.

Our liquids released;
consumed by life's tasks, pains and joys.
Emptied,
we become abandoned,
discarded,
broken.

By this action
we are freed.
We become open to roam the oceans,
the universe of souls,
being moved by the tides;
handling conflicts,
experiencing the flow of existence.

In time, we return to shore,
no longer that shiny empty shell.
Now we are scattered across the great expanse.
Each separate piece,
still part of the whole,

but on different journeys
to different shores.

As beach glass,
new experiences still await.
Weathered now – a satin finish,
We are somehow more unique,
more beautiful.

Dance of Light and Shadows

The beauty of light and shadows is that it allows one to get a sense of depth. Shadows and reflections, the movement of light, opens life to so many interpretations. There are so many currents and vibrations to life. Our eyes and minds tend to focus only on the main visual events taking place at any moment – the walking person, the moving car, the swaying tree. But in reality these scenes are only the tip of the iceberg of the magic of life unfolding before us at every moment.

Every now and then something inside me makes me delve into these eddies off the main stream of life. To become observant of the shadows of the idle objects in the background; to absorb the nuances of light as it dances behind the stillness. The poet in me realizes that shadows are so very important – they add to the depth and vastness of life. There is so much life in the stillness:

Still Life

My eyes at times
capture simple scenes
at the edge of the field of action.
The table after dinner;
before dinner;
with no dinner,
just random objects on it.

A mind picture,
a modern day version
of an old still life,
as painted by those Dutch masters.

A still life with fruit,
by itself shows no action.
There is a sense of permanence in that.
There is also a narrative
that can be weaved,
true or fabled.
Objects at the fringe
absorb the story of events.
It is there waiting to be interpreted
not from a book, report or narrative,
but from the objects themselves.

There is often poetry,
A rhythm
in their placement,
in their lines,
in their relationship to other objects
on the table.

It is not revealed overtly.
These stories are revealed
in hints of fragrance,
an idly placed object,
a discarded item.
These stories are part of the matrix of life,
displayed in small bits and segments to the mind's eye.

A still life to the eye
Can open the mind to the unintentional,
which to the quiet mind
reveals the intentional.

I relish being in the warmth and brilliance of light, but I am observant of the shadows cast. I find life so much more than the standard eight-color crayon box; much more even than the 64 or 128 color sets. A page cannot contain the number of zeros required to account for all the different colors and possible shading variations of color that life reflects, but a poem or art or music sometimes can. Why? Because art touches upon the infinite: the soul, the heart, our center of wonderment; the home of our beginning.

The beauty of a painted flower is intensified by its interplay of light and shadows. The poet paints an image with a palate of words, mixing the colors and symbolisms to create the right tints. The composer uses the possibilities and interplay of pitch, sound, and scale to create a sound poem. The artist uses shape, color, and shadows to create a sense of movement or stillness.

The potentials are boundless; variations on the theme endless. Those who open up to the infinite of their soul force are continually exploring the deepness of life. In the stillness, the beauty of shadows and the dance of light is there to be absorbed.

Accepting that Some Things Happen in Their Own Good Time

Learning to Accept Acceptance

Acceptance is our perfect gift to self. You might think that at this stage in life things would be going along just ducky, and that I would be a go-with-the-flow, smell-the-flowers sort of person. For the most part, you would be wrong. It seems that much of life is filled with self-made conflicts over learning to accept life on life's terms. It seems it is almost impossible at times to surrender to the moment.

So much of our self-made anguish is created by our resistance to the truths of the events in our lives. So much freedom is possible when one learns to release the need to control, and begin to accept life on life's terms.

This holds especially true for our thoughts. Trying to repress them is a waste of personal energy. We end up putting ourselves into personal internal conflict. Hey, when you get down to it, a thought is a thought is a thought. They are just reflections of the hidden intimacies of your life. Thoughts are not necessarily good or bad; they just are. They do not need to be judged, rated and categorized.

The good thing about thoughts is they do not require action. A so-called bad thought does not have to be acted upon. It can be thought and then just as easily released with no action required. Not to worry though; one thought will soon be followed by another, which can also not be acted upon. Worrying about "bad" thoughts and self-castrating one's self over them only leads to repression, a stopping of the flow of life. The net result of such action will be depression, a state of non-existence in our present moment world.

I consider myself a non-controlling type of person. This is a self-created myth. When in a controlling mode, acceptance is not possible. Present moment living is not possible. The internal self becomes dammed up. Thoughts end up swirling around in a vortex within, creating ill-ness, sickness of spirit, body and stress. It leads to a condition known as dis-ease. In such a state one is not at ease with one's self.

Feelings are very present moment. If not hindered or controlled, they flow in and they will flow out. Trying to control or not accept what "is" does not change what "is". Accepting allows events and thoughts to flow freely. Acceptance empowers; resistance does not.

Acceptance is very present moment living. It is not forever. It is only for the moment. It does not mean we have to approve or disapprove of thoughts and feelings. Acceptance means we allow ourselves to feel what is happening in the present moment. We then have the ability to act upon such thoughts.

The poet in me often deals with this process of accepting what is. Writing and creating helps develop a sense of self-trust, self-acceptance, and self-love. Love of self allows one the freedom and joy to love and accept others free from the boundaries of controlling. In freedom there is love, but I still find myself saying to myself "But when?" I guess I need to accept that this will happen when it happens, in other words, in its own good time:

In Its Own Good Time

Plants sprout when it's time.
Animals hibernate, awake, and mate
at their right time.
Planets move,
tides rise and ebb,
the seasons come and go,
all in their own good time.

It is only we, the collective "I"s,
that want things to happen
when we want them to happen.
We rush.
I rush.
Nature does not rush.

There are plans and symmetries
that function perfectly well
without any input from me.
Interfering creates disorder.

When will I learn
that there is order to the chaos

I think I see?
Things go the way that
they are meant to.
Answers come when they come.

Forcing doesn't seem to solve a whole lot.
Sometimes it is best to step away.
Time is only a concept that I create anyway.
It has no real importance.

When will I accept this simple fact?
I guess that it will happen
in its own good time.

Anam Cara and the Concept of Soul Friendship

There is a form of friendship that the word "friendship" is inadequate to describe. The concept goes much deeper than that. It is much nobler of spirit; more intense. "Anam Cara" is the term that comes closest in expressing it.

"Anam Cara" is a Celtic phrase, which translates into "soul friend". Poetry and song tend to be the best format for expressing it – the nobility of friendship:

By the Isle of Anam Cara

Anchored off the leeward side
of the Isle of Anam Cara
lies the vessel of my soul.

As morning is conceived,
the darkness engulfing
the vessel of my soul,
is replaced
by the beauty of innocent dawn.

As the dragons create sky fires,
my eyes grow accustomed
to the faint hint of early
light.

My mind's eye
in the darkness of isolation,
begins to pilot my soul
through the shoals of
self-doubts,
to touch against you,
my rock,
my soul's friend,
you are my isle,
my Anam Cara.

I was first introduced to this phrase in a book of the same name by *John O'Donahue*. His book is an eloquent song-poem on the soul beauty of this form of relationship. A life-poem on the true meaning of intimacy. With someone who is your *Anam Cara*, you are safe to reveal the hidden intimacies and feelings of your spirit. You are safe to share your innermost self, your mind's thoughts, and your heart. You can freely share with an *Anam Cara* the beauty of the divine light that flows through you. An *Anam Cara* is more than a bitch mate; someone to complain to about life's perceived problems. He or she is not your bar buddy, phone buddy, bathroom mirror buddy, but a person that you communicate with on a soul level.

An *Anam Cara* friendship has no need for convention or categorizing, since joining is on a soul level. The superficiality and the dressings of convention fall away. They have no place. Love of another's soul and spirit opens you to the flow of love.

Through loving and acceptance of another, you, in turn, can begin to fully love another as well as yourself – a perfect poem to life, and a true gift of the heart.

You are truly able to open up when in this state of soul love. You can experience happiness throughout your being. There is trust and understanding that does not need to be shared through spoken words. Between soul friends there is often psychic communication. The vessel of your soul finds safe harbor within the radiance and protective circle of another.

This act of love, not to be confused with sex, allows freedom of self – a blossoming of the spirit. Nourished by the light of divine love, the specialness of another, your spirit can blossom, and a life poem is created. A poem of words can only hint at the beauty of this level of sharing, intimacy and acceptance. But a heart that is open and sings with love can accept the gift of the perfect friendship.

How Many Angels Can You Get on a Pinhead?

To tell you the truth, I really have no idea how many angels can stand on the top of a pin. I never gave it much thought really. I like the concept of angels though. I like many of the artsy, cutesy renditions of them that you find in stores, card displays, knick-knack shops, etc.

The concept of flying is always very pleasing to the spirit. We all seem to love to be able to soar in the sky. The idea of being looked-out for and protected is also a very soothing and calming feeling, especially for that frightened child residing within all of us.

Let's face it, angels sell. Their personification as a most perfect representation of the human image within us with wings is uplifting. Say "angel", and one is most prone to think of those Madison Avenue versions of cherubs - laughing, bubbly baby-like, basically sexless in their depiction.

My impression of angels is far less humanized. I personally don't see angels as they are generally drawn by Madison Avenue. To me, angels are more a personification of the force of love, the living spirit of the universe that flows through all of us. To me there is a nurturing intelligence out there, and also, right here inside us. We are all part of it, even when we don't seem to have the foggiest idea of what any of this is all about. That doesn't matter really because whether we accept it consciously or not, we are still part of the whole.

It is a wonderful concept to hold onto especially when the "I" in me feels lonely. The fact is we are never alone. We may cut ourselves off from the flow of universal love, but that loving light never abandons us. It's there for us whether we accept it, reject it, realize it, or haven't a clue about it. Like those white corpuscles in our blood stream; they are a force that comes to our aid when we need it and begins to work its magic. It's like that inner voice that whispers from somewhere within our self-preservation system warning us to stop and not step into the street just as a speeding truck races by 2 inches from the curb.

We don't know why, and we don't really understand how, but even the most skeptical of us realizes that there is something that unconsciously protects us. Angels are a perfect personification of this force of love.

You know angels may look exactly like we've been representing them all these centuries. They may move about us on a higher vibration level, spiritual entities with their own individual names and ID nameplates. Heck, angels may really look like toads, but that image doesn't sell greeting cards.

We humans tend to put what we have difficulty in understanding into human terms. It makes things easier to understand. Gabriel, Michael, and all those others may very well be card-carrying members of the Heaven Squad, and Lucifer, founding member of the Fallen Angel club.

It really doesn't matter if we have the names right, or that they really look like we tend to depict them. The bottom line is this – the force is real. How do I know this? There are angels in my life:

House of Broken Angels

I live in a house filled with angels.
I think most of us do.
Mine come in all shapes,
sizes and poses;
one is only a musical tune.

Angels touch my life
in very special ways.
I know that they are with me
throughout the course of my day.

Although life has been far from perfect,
at least to my way of thinking,
angels always seem to have been there for me,
to save from those really great falls.

How do I know?
It's easy.
All my angels are broken.
They've taken those big hits from life
that were meant to flatten me.

Broken wings, arms, and heads,
they all have had to be re-glued.
It's sort of a mini-hospital at my desk,
for these fallen comrades
in duty to my soul.

So, thank you angels,
one and all,
for caring for me every day.
I'll keep the glue handy!

Do You Live Your Dreams?

Do you still dream? Not the dreams of subconscious sleep, but the dreams of your heart's longings? Are you still willing to take a risk; look the fool; color outside the lines of your orchestrated coloring book of life? If so, then life is still an adventure. If not, you need to read no further. Either you have attained all your goals, or have meekly quit living life's adventures and are sitting quietly awaiting death, even if it is some 20-30 years away.

Living life in a holding pattern isn't living. It is "status quoing". Basically, it is you working at keeping everything seemingly unchanged.

Part of you should never want things to continually remain exactly the same. It is an illusion to think that they can. Subtle changes are always happening, and one day that illusion of stability will come apart and you will be left naked and alone wondering why.

We often stick with the familiarity of the everyday and 'sameness" out of fear; the fear of embracing each new morning as the beginning of a new adventure; as a chance to live our dreams, even before we might even consciously acknowledge that we even have a dream.

Remember the deepest longings of the soul are rarely concerned with the practicality of making mortgage payments, car payments, or making sure that lawn is cut before it gets too high. The deepest desires of your soul are concerned with freedom and what is important to your core being. It might not be what other's want, or society has seemingly prescribed for you. It is centered on what will bring you a sense of completeness and inner serenity. Age is not a curtailment to one's dreams.

I still have dreams to live; quests to follow; new dawns to greet with a sense of anticipation, and yes, maybe some fears, too. However, fear is not my ruler, and it should not be yours. Let your desire to live completely grow within you until it is greater than any self-made fears. Do not waste your life force falsely feeding fears. Get off your ass and get out on the floor of life. Get your feet moving. Dance and sing to your own songs of joyful life.

Lip-Synching to the Songs of Life

Are you still so fearful
that you cannot even lip-synch to the songs of life?
Where is that sense of adventure and wonderment
to stray from the beaten pathways of life
and pick wildflowers from the hillsides?
To close your eyes and soar on the back of a dragon
through the clouds chasing wisps of vanishing fairy dust;
to lick the morning dew from honeysuckle flowers;
to roll down a hill in childlike abandonment.

Why do we instead, refuse to free our silent voices;
open our chakras; close our eyes;
throw back our heads and sing;
sing the song of life with joy and freedom?

Why?

Hey, you know why.
We might make a mistake,
sing off-key, forget the tune.
So, at best, we only mouth the words, and
let the rest of the choir of life carry the hymn,
just like in church.

But wouldn't it be great,
if we found the courage and self-love
to release our energy from the clutches of our egos?
Free our voices to sing loudly and joyfully
the song of life, not giving a damn
how it sounds to others or our ego.

I dream one day to be totally free.
To lie on that hillside, and
compose my own life-tunes and words.
To ride on the back of that dragon,
sipping nectar from honeysuckles,
while filling the skies with my songs.

Checking My Saved Time Account of Life

I tried to check my account of time saved the other day. You know the one, the account where all the time we've saved over the years is kept. All that time that those labor savings devices and multi-tasking computers have shaved off the usual completion time. I mean it must have added up to a lot by now.

I realized that I never received a statement in the mail about this, so it must be on the computer somewhere. I went to the computer and tried to log in to SavedTime.com However, I had no idea what my password was. I tried "time" - no good. I tried "life" - NG to that one, too. I tried a half dozen more - no cigar. Then I had one of the "V-8" moments - You know, that moment when a person smacks his or her forehead and says "I could have had a V-8".

It hit me. Bingo! I had no password. In fact, there was no savedtime.com, no Amalgamated Bank of Time Saved. Nothing! All I had was a present moment - a NOW. And suddenly I realized that the hourglass of life seems to have a lot more sand in the bottom section than the top. Bummer!

What insight did this give me? It gave a lot, a real lot. You know, time is not for saving. Time, it seems, is for living. And it can't be done in the past or at compounded interest for some future date. It can only be done NOW.

So what is the purpose of this reflection? I guess it's this - Do the NOW thing , like now. For me it means that before my account gets closed out I need to spend more time living than saving. Postponing living in the present is definitely beginning not to be an option.

NOW is the only time I really have. I have got to stop waiting to live.

WAITING

Life is a waiting game at times.
It shouldn't be,
but it is.
Most of us tend to make it so.
Waiting for our proverbial ship to come in.
Waiting for our luck to change.
Waiting for Godot.
Waiting,
Waiting,
Waiting for things that will never be.

Waiting to make the big bucks;
to take that vacation;
waiting for that promotion;
waiting for retirement,
Hell, waiting for death even.

In the military they have a phrase "Hurry up and wait".
So very appropriate.

Why do we do this to ourselves?
The animals in the fields don't.
Flowers don't.
The simplest of creatures
have no need to.
They are always in the "now".

Even when trying to be still,
the mind rarely clears.
I'm sick of waiting for my **Present**.
Why do I do this to myself?
I'm still waiting for the answer.

Monsters Under the Bed

Yes, as scary and upsetting as it might sound, there are monsters under the bed... and in the closets, and under the cellar staircase. There are nightmares in this world.

Monsters Under the Bed

I know monsters hide under the bed.
That's why I have a platform one.
I know that open closets are gateways
for goblins and such to sneak into your room at night.
That's why I always make sure that mine
is securely shut tight.

I still dread the scary creatures
who hide under the cellar staircase.
What if the lights go out
when I am in the basement!
Then there's the roaring furnace monster
that can open the furnace door
and drag me to a fiery death!

God knows I've lost track of all the creatures
that lurk outside in the dark,
hiding among the branches, brambles
and shrubs.

This especially holds true when evening comes
and the vampires come out to feed;
not to mention the rotting corpses
from "Creature Features" that arise
from those Stephen King unholy cemeteries
hidden at Indian massacre sites.

But most of all I am afraid of the real monsters
who dwell within the realm of my mind.
These demons, dragons, skeletons, ghouls and such
are always with me.
I can't hide from them,
they always know where I am,
since they are created by me.

Crosses and sacred amulets avail me not.
No, these monsters are the ones I fear the most.
Only the light of self-acceptance and truth
can save me from them, but…
I am so afraid of the light!

The good news of sorts is that we created these monsters. And as their creators, we can be their un-creators. Our nightmares are manifested by us to express feelings, fears, etc. that need to be felt and processed.

The better news about all of this is our dreams can be changed. We can swim with the dolphins in the oceans of the sky basking under a warming sun. We don't have to dwell in the realms of darkness and oozing scary things. We are our own dream machines. Sounds wonderful on some level, right? It is wonderful. You can let the poet sing the songs of the spirit with verses from the heart. They, you, can release the inner child from the dungeon of fears.

Our nightmares are an outlet for feelings we've chosen not to process completely. So, too, are many of the illnesses that we have. Nightmares, diseases, illnesses are some of the ways that we process unfelt feelings. We may numb ourselves to these unprocessed feelings in our waking hours, but that doesn't make them go away. Repressed feelings and emotions will show up in other ways. The nightmares will come.

Our dreams are our guides for the spirit. We need to honor them. Allow the natural process to flow. Let the poet express what the spirit feels. Fear need not be the foundation of our life or dreams. Foundations built upon fear are false footings. Life is meant to be lived, not avoided out of fear. Dreams are there to give us guidance in magical ways. Nightmares will give us guidance, too, except the methods used are very unsettling.

Fears are a natural part of living, but they are meant to be fleeting – warnings, telling us, that some action needs to be taken, immediately. Fears avoided, or suppressed, are the growing fields of nightmares. Nightmares are very empathetic messengers – we tend to give them our immediate attention, especially if our heart is left beating rapidly. These messengers tell us that some action needs to be taken. The poet in us cannot ignore them. Life isn't all flowers and hillsides. When I write about my nightmares, it helps.

Life and Love are 4 Letter Words, Too

We are all part of this wonderful experience called "life". We often seem to do our best not to live it on life's terms though, cursing and swearing at our results. No matter, if we willingly accept life, or cover it over with layers and layers of denial and games, in the end, life is still life. We need to learn to deal with it, especially in the present moment.

We are surrounded by so many stimuli. We have the opportunity to pick and choose what we take in and process. That is why several people can be subjected to basically the same situation, the same stimulation, and each one will have a different reaction - from feelings of joy and contentment to total despair and hopelessness. The stimuli are the same, the reaction different. The reason all of this happens within each of us is that a person who has faith in the goodness of purpose about life can see flowers growing on a hillside even on a stormy rainy day. A person whose four-letter vocabulary is full of "love", "hope", and "good" creates a poetry of life that is filled with happiness, acceptance and inner peace.

For a person whose four letter vocabulary is filled with those street-wise favorites we all seem to know sees life differently. To such a person with a closed heart and spirit, who doesn't readily see the beauty of life, its poetry; to a person who doesn't see the flowers, but sees garbage, life is seen with a closed heart and spirit. To such a person happiness is not a normal condition, but only a nebulous goal that will always remain unattainable. Such a life has no flowing, only struggles.

Dreams are windows into the realms of possibilities. A life that is flowing, a heart that is filled with love and hope, is a life of with unfolding dreams. Life is an adventure, not a task. Laughter and love are the substances that nourish the soul. Pain exists, but is accepted for what it is, one of the many temporary experiences possible to us, not an inevitable destination.

On those down days when my mind seems filled with four-letter expletives, life stops. On those other days filled with those four-letter words "love" and "hope", life flows. Life is full of choices. The choice of what kind of day to live is always mine. In this life I create the poetry in my life. As another four-letter day unfolds, I have the choice to pick which words to live by, and so do you!

Choose wisely!

Life Is a 4-Letter Word Called Love

We are one with the Universe,
coursing upon Life's river.
We are one with the all,
Alpha and Omega,
the beginning and the end.

We are a gift of our Loving Lord.
We all spring forth from the
well of Pure Love.

Together we form a forest of
special uniqueness;
each a leaf on the Tree of Life.
The same spring of Love
nurtures our roots.

By staying in the pure light
of Love,
absorbing God's blessings
that flow from this well,
we can all flower in love.

We are each spiritual blossoms;
heavenly wildflowers
blooming in love.
Life is love.

Life's a Beach! Especially for the Young at Heart!

As they say "Life's a beach"! There's a lot of truth to this statement. To me there is something special and soul-touching about being at the ocean. It's always different; yet somewhat always unchanged. In many respects it is our eternal mother.

All that deep soul-stuff aside, being at the beach and ocean is just plain old F-U-N. But to truly enjoy the beach you must see it through the eyes of a child. Small kids just know instinctively how to understand the true essence of the shoreline. They explore, play, create fantasy worlds and build sand castles all at the same time.

You want to get the kids (and yourself) away from the TV, video games and cries of "I'm bored". Just pile everyone into the car and head to the beach. If you're old, the same guidance applies, except you might need to substitute "work" for "video games", if that works better for your imagination.

The ocean always calls to me. The child in me embraces it. And even now that I'm older, I still enjoy the whole experience by watching the little children at play along the shoreline. It hasn't changed much since I was a child and I bet the same was true for my parents and theirs.

Do yourself a favor soon and get to the beach. Yes put some sun screen on first though. Take in the majesty of the ocean; calm your inner voices and practice doing "nothingness" for a while. If you have a problem doing this, just watch the children and you will remember!

Beach Secrets

Beaches are one of the reasons
you have children,
or maybe it is somewhat the other way around.
But, no matter,
little children know the secrets
of a beach.

If you really want to feel the magic
of the beach
you must see with the eyes of a child.
Little children see the secret world of life,
the flow of vibrations
along the shoreline;
each shell a treasure with its own story;
their beauty missed by adult eyes.

Screeches of glee;
falling down in the surf.
Joyful screams as little legs
run from incoming waves.

So proud to be on their own,
they have one eye hunting
for the next incoming wave;
the other on their parents.

Sand in the coolie is a natural part
of the beach experience,
the magic of the beach.

How many adults can say that?

My Resolutions for the New Year as a 9 Year Old

OK, most people make resolutions for the New Year, and most resolutions are forgotten a week or so later. I have some thoughts for the upcoming year. First off, it's got to better than the year before. I have a more positive attitude for this New Year that's for sure. And, hopefully the Mayan calendar is off by a few million years.

I've been making lists of goals for years now - 10 or 12. Some years my goals looked more like a business plan than a living plan, but they always had a positive aspect to them, and I tried to make sure that they appeared realistically attainable to me. I may still do that this year, but I'm trying to concentrate on one positive goal - Making this a year of transformation. I originally was going to say "transition", but "transformation" has a more "already accomplished, living it now" aspect to it. I don't want to strive this year, I want to be there already and live my new life from day 1, or day 2 anyway. All the years that I've lived coming up to this point were my transition years. Now is the time to "BE" transformed, not plan for it.

Anyway, one of my life style transformations that I will be living this year is writing more. Not thinking about what to write, but actually getting my thoughts down on paper (OK or on the computer, but I'll print a paper copy out anyway, because we Baby Boomers for the most part still relate to paper. It has more magic and power to it than a computer screen and I think will last longer and not be lost in the great computer crash of 2014 or 2016 or whenever).

But instead of sharing my adult Baby Boomer Resolutions now, I thought, thought I, what kind of resolutions would I make if I was still a little kid, and believe me part of me is still that little kid, and hopefully will forever be.

My New Year's Resolutions at the Age of 9

What will I resolve in this New Year?
In this year that I turn 9.
(With fingers crossed behind my back)
This is what I'll do.

I'll go to bed when mom and dad say.
I won't whine all the time
when I don't get my way.
I'll eat what mom cooks,
even if it's brussel sprouts!
(no gagging at the table, anyway).

I'll clean my room at least once a week
(once a month probably).
I'll shut the lights off when I leave a room
so I don't have to hear
"We don't own stock in Con Ed, you know!"

I'll do my homework everyday
as soon as I get home
or when my favorite show is over,
(I have a lot of favorite shows!)
I won't pick my nose in public and
wipe it on my pants anymore.

I'll brush my teeth more than 5 seconds
and not squeeze the tube only at the top.
I won't leave the refrigerator door open all the time,
nor put back the milk container
when it only has a drop.

I'll share more with my brothers and sister
(but only if they share with me).
I won't leave my comics and baseball cards
all over the floor.
Who knows, they might be valuable someday.

But most of all
I vow to be better and nicer
in the coming year!
(just like I promised the year before!)

You know looking at this list again, I think I still need to work on some of these resolutions – just a little anyway! Have a super year! It all starts with attitude! The rest will fall in place.

Mom's Day Ramblings

Well Happy Mom's Day! (It sounds more personal than "mother"). Mom. It's something we all have - a Mom. And when she is, or was, on active service for us, it was, or is, mom's day every day.

As a baby boomer our mom's probably pretty old by now, or have already passed over, like my mom has. Just so you know, I am a dad so I did my part to increase the ranks of motherhood. When I was young, moms were the moms and the dads were the dads (remember "Just wait till your father gets home!"). When I got older the lines of responsibility between the sexes became more fluid, which is probably a good thing. As a "Mr. Mom" myself I might not be able to breast feed (scary visual there) but I can change a diaper with the best of them; cook a meal; be the taxi service; and bandage-up and kiss a booboo.

As I mentioned, my mom passed away not too long ago. We (the kids) were by her bedside during a vicious snowstorm. It sucked watching her slip away. It was very painful. My mom hardly ever complained and she had multiple ailments and health issues for years. Her mind might have wandered at times, but she definitely still had all her wits about her.

Anyway I wish all the moms out there and those that serve in the capacity of motherhood and nurturing a great Mother's Day, not just this one day, but every day.

One thing I will mention about my mom are her eyes. Even as the end neared her eyes were so clear, not filmy or clouded over, and they were so blue.

Mom's Blue Eyes

She had the bluest of eyes.
Even in old age
they never clouded over.
She could see what others could not;
she could see wonders.

Her skin was an alabaster white,
reminding one of those ancient Greek statues
that you can seemingly see a few layers into.
Usually cool to the touch,
she radiated warmth.

She rarely complained.
Her body was frail;
there were pains,
but she never dwelled on them.

From her couch in her favorite room,
she took journeys of wonder
with old friends and family.
She would re-visit places
she knew from decades past,

as the sun slowly set
outside of her window.

Farewells are rarely easy.
But if your time is here
than it is best to say one's goodbyes
surrounded by family.
Mom did.

The days go on,
the emptiness is filled
with memories of happier times.
Then there is always
the vision of your face and eyes;
those eyes that were so blue.

Take Time in Life to go a Whimsey

Life being what it is and is not, it is very important that we all carve out some time to just wander about. Just open our inner eye and take in the usually unseen magical moments taking place, while we're busy taking care of the so-called "important" stuff. I even have a whimsical name for such adventures - whimsey, or, if you prefer, whimsy. I prefer whimsey, so whimsey it is for me.

A "whimsey" is much more than what can be called a whimsical moment. This is using "whimsey" as a noun rather than an adjective of life. I first heard this word used this way when I saw the Oscar Wilde play, "The Importance of Being Earnest". It was at a performance put on at Princeton University. My son, Brendan, played Algernon Moncrieff (as an aside all the female roles were played in drag and most of the audience didn't know this until curtain calls). Whenever Algernon needed to get away from it all, he would either go see his imaginary friend, Bunbury, who always seemed to be on his deathbed, or just go on a whimsey.

I immediately fell in love with this word - whimsey. It seems to be the perfect word for a perfect need. A need to just get away and, well, just be. You know when things get to be too much, or life becomes too stale, just go out on a whimsey. Likewise, when life starts putting up too many detour signs then learn to just go along with the flow and enjoy the scenery. Look upon such occasions as an opportunity to go on a whimsey.

We should all seriously consider being unserious and find magic in each moment. Let the Fates direct your journey. Become a free spirit and the rest of life will flow along much more easily.

Whimsey

Sometimes events of the day
necessitate that my body and soul
escape the daily tedium.
Get away from TV, newspapers,
blaring radios;
away from bills, chores;
the grind of life in general.

At such moments, it's time to go on
a whimsey.
I know that it's somewhat of an old fashioned
word,
A little bit out of step with the times,
But it is the right word.

Yep, it's very gingham and lace
for a sandlot baseball kid at heart,
but a whimsey it is.
A brief, no-direction at all,
fantasy adventure -
dream fields,

sunny skies,
blue outlined sculptured clouds,
honeysuckle scents,
babbling, unseen waters,
a hint of distant ocean's calling.

A whimsey refreshes the spirit,
relaxing tensions.
recharging,
renewing,
revitalizing.

Whether in this dimension,
or another state of existence,
when I can go a'whimseying along
on my whimsical way,
a smile will come to my face;
a dance to my step;
a tune to my lips.

Aaaahhh…
to stop the car;
walk in a field;
and take a whimsey.
Child eyes open
to butterfly moments.

Thanksgiving and Black Friday

Thanksgiving Day and Black Friday, I sometimes wonder which one means more. From a strictly economical point of view - Black Friday wins hands down. After buying a turkey, some pies, pastries, etc., and maybe a few Hallmark Cards, there aren't too many other revenue flows from this day. I sometimes think it is all just a lead-in to next day - BLACK FRIDAY!

All the TV commercials are about Buy - Buy - Buy!! This is the great American mantra I guess. It's a shame somewhat because Thanksgiving is a folksy kind of day: family-oriented and mostly a good vibrations event. Even if we (those of European stock, anyway) did screw the Native Americans out of their land, and forgetting that the Puritans were a strict "My Way or the Highway to Hell" religious group, a day of thanksgiving and family can't be all a bad thing.

Anyway I just want to wish all a relaxing comfortable day. And rest up: Remember! Black Friday is an American Holy Day of Obligation.

Black Friday
Holy Day of Obligation

On today,
Thanksgivings Day,
so many images
of shopping and bargains bombard me.
What to get Aunt So and So,
Little Dimple Eyes, the pets,
and everyone else on my sacred list?
For the Day of Gifts and Guilt
is quickly coming up next month.

The impending storm of Black Friday
is on the horizon.
I tremble at its approach,
and what it means.
I know that I will be caught up
in this tempest.
I shall shop till I drop.

But this year I shall shop smarter!

I will shop for Light,
for hope, and
Oh no! not that trite phrase
"World Peace"
Better than that,

I will shop for intimacy,
for intimacy of the spirit.
I will avoid the malls,
and visit a suffering soul,
bringing a gift of Light
all wrapped up.

Tears

Tears - we shed them for many reasons. When we were kids running, we fell and scraped our knees - tears. When someone close to us gets injured or dies – tears. A national or worldwide tragedy occurs – tears. Even when we see a very emotional movie – tears; we don't call them tearjerkers for nothing. I cried during "Bambi", "ET," and "A Christmas Carol" (the old B/W version starring Alastair Sim). I can cry when someone sings a beautiful emotional song. Heck, I can shed tears during a commercial.

In the deepest reaches of our sorrow – tears; those are the worst kind. There is almost no consolation; the agony of the loss and sorrow grips your entire being.

But there is another type of tear - a soft tear, a tear that is a gift of the heart, a package of happiness in liquid form. These are spontaneous gifts. No forethought is given, no pre-planning; they just come. These are not to be confused with so-called "crocodile" tears. There is nothing phony about them. They're definitely not onion tears, either.

These tears are manifestations of joy.

A birth, a lost child found, a loved one returning from the horrors of war walking through the door. These are the most precious and sacred of gifts. And only a heart that is true and open can create such self-gifts.

More than anything else tears are what make us human.

Tears

Sometimes there is more joy in one tear
Than in 10 bellyfuls of laughter;
more love
than in any hug of happiness;
more intensity
than in a 100 movie endings.

Only a tear can capture
the essence of joy,
encapsulated in a drop of soul water.

A tear is a simple gift
of true self,
offered from the soul
through the heart.

Tears of sorrow
are for losses.
Tears of joy
are for joinings.

A tear can be a gift of unselfishness;
a way to share with another,
even if done in darkness of the night.

A tear of joy
is a ceremony of love.
it makes us human
in the most god-like of way.

The Lost Art of Catching Snow Flakes on Your Tongue

It snowed the other day in the morning for a little bit. It was that slowly drifting floating down kind of snow. Not a blizzard; not a blinding inferno of whiteness and cold. It felt well, comfortable. It didn't last long, but for a while it became very quiet outside.

Sometimes snow has a way of bringing a peaceful kind of silence; softening everything around. The lines of separation between objects become vague and slowly disappear. There is a continuum of oneness, a continuum of whiteness. If one were in a forest or quiet field it would be a moment for a deep spiritual experience. But for me it was a quiet moment waiting for a light to change going from an off street turning onto a busy one. So the moment didn't last but it was enough to connect, if only for a moment. It refreshed my spirit before it all changed to rain and became colder.

We all need moments like this. When you find that you are in one - stop for a moment; expand your senses; take in the experience.

Oh! one other thing, the most important observation in retrospect, I saw a bunch of little kids waiting at a bus stop; more than a 1/3 had their tongues out to catch the flakes. They were one with the experience. Not one older kid or adult did it. That's a shame somewhat. I guess we become conditioned to miss the magic moments of life; that's a tragedy. Don't let it happen to you!

Snow Child

It's snowing! It's snowing!
The kid in me cries for joy.

Look at the million billion flakes.
Are they all different, or all the same?
What the heck do I care,
as long as it sticks!

I sure hope it's good packing snow;
that's the best kind
for making snowballs and snowmen
and play-scapes of pure white.

Snow makes the air quieter.
Silence prevails my landscape,
except for some skidding cars
and snowplows scraping away.

Oh! I don't mind walking in that
slip-sliding sort of way on such
a snow white beautiful day.
Well, as long as I don't take a header.

I don't care if anyone looks
when I stick my tongue out
to catch the swirling flakes.
They look like teeny-tiny fairies.

Oh don't worry, I still remember the rule
about not eating yellow snow.
But that white fresh stuff
sure tastes mighty-mighty good.

Yes, my glasses freeze up,
as the snow melts on them.
But I still see well enough
to enjoy this special day.

No more snow days for me anymore.
That's a shame.
But that's part of the rules
in this growing-up game.

My hair, what's still there,
blends nicely with the snow.
I even been heard to say now
"You think this is bad,
remember the snow of _____"

I might have aged, but I'm not old.
In fact, I will never grow old,
as long as I love the snow.

The Weight of Joy

One thing that I am realizing in doing this "life" thing is that when I am in a joyous state things just feel lighter, brighter, open and moving, translucent even. There is an aura of light and energy around everything and everyone; just like in one of those Kirlian photographs.

Life flows. I flow. You flow. We are all part of the universal flow of energy. When I am in "the flow" I don't need to rush so much; try so hard; force myself to think so much; because everything will seemingly just flow. There is a sense of unity to everything.

However, all too often life feels heavy, somber, dark, slow. Movement is like trying to walk through a quagmire; everything drags or stagnates. When you feel heavy your mind often races at the speed of light, or worse, goes into some dark recess where nothing flows. How does one get out of such a state? By becoming weightless!

The most liberating way to live life is to live it in a state of weightlessness. Lift the pressure sitting on your chest, on your shoulders, your mind, your heart. Learning to go weightless will allow life's energy to flow around and through you again. One of the quickest ways to weightlessness is joy.

Joy is a state of being that permeates your entire body. It's a state of energy; it's a form of light. Look for those moments in your life. Attune your body and being to be receptive to them. It will require you to quiet the self-defeating mind talk that so often takes place.

Joy doesn't necessarily come with a big price tag either. It is always around you. It was a natural part of your life as a small child, before life came along and buried it. It can become a natural part of your life again. All you need to do is clear an open space in your life and allow it in. Learn how to live life in a state of joyous weightlessness and flow with life, not fight it. Start little, but just start. It is never too late.

Take a deep cleansing breath to open a space within you then let the miracle of joyousness engulf you. Become weightless and fly…

The Weight of Joy

I don't understand this "joy" thing.
So very often it doesn't seem
to have much substance to it;
just light, sun, air, transparency,
open skies to the eternal.

Now sadness, despair, melancholia
has substance to it.
You can feel it weighing down
upon you.

Joy has only a "now" feeling to it,
no future or past,
it is a present moment feeling.
It is basically beyond my control
when it overtakes me,
and what makes it more dangerous
it can be very contagious.

You see it exhibited a lot by kids and dogs.
You can educate and control it out of children.
You can beat it out of dogs.
You can ignore it within yourself,
but,
you must be very diligent,
or it can come sneaking back into your life,
when you least expect it.
And we can't have that,
now can we?

There Are No Ordinary Moments

Well today is my daughter's birthday, which got me to thinking, and sometimes that can be a dangerous thing.

Today is a special day for her, for me, for her mother, but when you really start thinking about it all – every day is a special day. And every day is made up of moments, and when you analyze it (if that is really necessary when you think about it) the most important part of our lives is not the date or anniversary or celebration. It is not even the day and I'm including this present day. It is the moment we are in - this present moment. That's it! 10-4 - Over and Out!

Here's the magic seed of life in a nutshell. Everything that we do; everything that has happened, and, the Good Lord willing, everything that will happen in the future will happen in the "Present Moment". And it is a shame that we let too many of them escape our notice thinking about this and that, or whatever else Mr. Ego has got going on in our minds to take our attention away from the fact that I got a present moment here right in front of me, and I better enjoy it.

Yes, there will be another moment along in a moment but I have this perfectly good present moment that I should be enjoying right now.

Happy birthday dear daughter! And happy birthday to my sons, and to all the sons and daughters, mothers and fathers, and grandparents out there. Thank you for reminding me of the most precious gift any of us have: Our Present Moments. Isn't that why they call it "Present"?

Because it is! And each moment is never ordinary. Each one is extraordinary!!

No Ordinary Moments

Treat every moment as special;
it is.
Treat every moment as sacred;
it is so.

Present moments
are gifts to ourselves;
to be totally engulfed in,
enjoyed.

There are no ordinary moments.

Notice the quality of your breath;
inhale the uniqueness of the present moment.
Seek not an ending;
there are none really.

Spirals and circles
beyond our understanding
keep us continually in the Present.

Be open to receive all things;
embrace the Light.
Let your spirit breathe.
Be one with the vitality of the Now.

There are no ordinary moments.

Tree Forts - Portal Back to Youth

Boy, as I kid, I was partner in many tree forts. I think I only fell out of one; came close a lot more times, but I was more agile in those days.

Why am I mentioning tree forts? I saw the remnants of one in a tree in a lot not too long ago. They used to be a common sight, but there's not very much undeveloped land on Long Island any more, and almost none in Queens, where I grew up. It's a shame really, tree forts were part of the male maturation process (cool word, huh, but it fits).

Anyway, seeing the tree fort platform through the trees gave me pause to think and relive some old memories. So anyway, (like that word, so transitional) I wrote this poem about tree forts.

My Tree Fort

I had one in my kid years;
well, more like "we" had one, really;
built by a bunch of kids, variations of me.
It was a real tree fort,
constructed from odd scrapes
of found and "borrowed" wood,

complete with shaky ladder steps
nailed into the side of the tree.
along with a special rope tow
for bringing up supplies.

Before the differences between boys and girls were known,
or cared about, really,
we had this golden rule,
which was strictly observed,
"No Girls Allowed"
a tree fort was sacred
male ground.

But,

"Wo-Wo" books were allowed,
because the mysteries of a woman's breast
caused wonderful stirrings in our bodies,
although we really had no idea what all this difference
really meant then.

You know, certain rites of childhood
should remain unchanged.
Secret clubs and tree forts are an absolute necessity.
Places where childhood thoughts can be shared;
dreams dreamt,
pains from the world of adults
nurtured.
Imagination needs to be given free reign
up in the kingdom of birds and leaves.

Why am I thinking this now?

I was driving past an old lot,
a fragment of still undeveloped land,
and caught a glimpse
between the leaves of an old tree
of the remnants of a tree fort.

And I remembered,
I remembered.

"Yes But" or just plain old "But"…

If not for the "buts" in my life…

There are some real nasty words that should not be used in gentile conversation, or in our own private mind-talk. For example, there's the popular 4-letter one - "Can't": like I can't exercise today because I have to watch my house plants grow, or I can't work/play at doing what I really want to do in life because _____ [fill in blank: not enough money, my job, my kids, my dog, my fears (real reason).] Hey! No Guts! No Glory!

Then there is that real show-stopper "BUT", or the hyphenated version "Yes-But".

"But" is what we say when we ignore our own good advice. "Yes-But" is what we use when someone gives us good advice, and we give our good (????) reason (what follows after "but') why we're not going to do it.

I've lived my life filled with too many "buts". You know it would have been better if my mom had washed my mouth out with soap when I said "but" rather than "shit". A life filled with "buts" is an unfulfilled one, when you get down to it I should just use the shortened version of the word – BS - self BS, at that.

An unhappy life is a life filled with too many "buts". A life lived in some stagnate limbo is a life filled with too many "buts" - roadblocks, self-erected ones. A life filled with "buts" prevents you/me from reaching the goals of "Yes I can!"

Still want to live your dream? You can! I can! All one has to do is get off your butt and work your "buts" off. (Bad, I know, but you get the idea!).

Mountain of But

I planned to live the life of my dreams.
I always wanted it; still do;
however, I haven't yet.
Why?
It lies on the other side of the Mountain,
the Mountain of But,
across the sea of the same name.

It is only a tomorrow or two away,
but, alas I dwell in the land of "yesterdays",
and "could have beens".
I kind of let my "todays" drift on away,
as I dream about the wonders and joys
I will experience when I cross the mountain;
swim the sea.

You see I still seem to dwell in the realm
of the Wizard of Buts,
who has control
of all that follows the word "but".

He magically lives within me.

When I say to myself
I can do this!
Here is my goal!
Yes, I can.
The wizard but waves his wand
and the spell of "but" stills the moment.

So many barriers of nothingness
prevent my own happiness.
I listen to my wizard
I see how high the mountain is,
how wide the waters of doubt.

The realm of fulfillment
is there
all I need to do is take the pathway of Yes,
which is right before me,
but I still fail to see it.

"Buts" are so powerful
when we listen to their magical enchantments.

Sing the Children's Song of Laughter

Laughter - we need more of it in our daily lives. You want to be healthier - laugh. You want to attract friends and influence people - laugh, naturally laugh. It is estimated that children laugh 300-400 times a day; adults 15 or so. Why is that?

It is because as adults we tend to use our brain first to comprehend what is happening and to ascertain the "humor" of a situation or comment. Then, and only then, if what we see or hear passes our "humor" test, will we laugh. This is called the mind to body model or the Humor model. It relies on our ability to understand what we consider funny and amusing. The problem with this model---it does not guarantee if a person will laugh. It is dependent on conditions like a sense of humor, the state of mind and what we deem is the quality of the external stimulus. This sounds somewhat complicated. Right?

The Childlike model of laughter takes the mind basically out of the equation and replaces it with how our body feels. Observe children-- they laugh the most while playing. Their laughter comes straight from the body and does not make use of any intellectual humor litmus test of the brain. The significant feature of this model is that the person actively participates in laughter and humorous activities instead of being a passive participant. Get the picture? Moving and laughter go together.

You can stimulate laughter just by moving your body and acting playful like a child. Think about it for a moment. When people are happy, they are more animated and expressive. When people are sad, they move less and are not very expressive—their bodies are sad and depressed. Want to be happy? Listen to your body more? Don't think and analyze. Do and Live. Be spontaneous. Be open to the flow of the universe. Just be in the moment!

Wow, little kids got it right. Just move and laugh. It will lead to a healthier, happier you!

Sing the Children's Song

I keep hearing this tune in my head.
To me it's the most beautiful music
I've ever heard.
We all know the words,
if "words" is the correct word?
I wonder if any of this song has words,
or a real tune for that matter;
but it is certainly music;
music to my heart.
It is the sound
of children's laughter,
the most beautiful music there is.

See I told you
we all know the words,
the tune,
the music.
It is the music of pure innocence
and total joy.
Listen to the children laugh -
full,
real,
completely consuming.

We need to sing along
with the children more.
We need to bring laughter
back into our lives.

Is a Garden Ever Dead?

Does a garden ever die? I would say not. Oh it may look bleak and dead in the middle of winter, but life is there; dormant perhaps, but there.

It's like those damn mosquitoes and small flying bugs. Right after a terrible winter when you get one of those sunny days and there's snow still on the ground and you know everything is going to re-freeze that night, you look around and there they are - Bingo right in your face.

It's amazing. How do they survive? How do we survive after an emotional winter of no love and loss? We just do; most of us anyway. Give us a warm day of love and sun and we spring back to life, just like those flying terrors; just like that frozen garden ground.

Be alert! Look for the signs. They might be small, but they are there.

Life is resilient, just like that garden. Death does come, but it is immediately replaced by life. Life is living love, and when you really get down to it the only real force is love. It is the moving energy. It is a life force that permeates everything.

Just wait - that "dead" garden will spring back to life at the blink of an eye. Then all you have to do is cultivate it and weed, of course. Like our lives - we cultivate and weed, and we eventually share in the bounty.

So is a garden ever dead? I think I just answered my own question.

IS A GARDEN EVER DEAD?

When the flowers are gone
is a garden still there?

Or does the bloom of the flowers
give it its life?

I think not.

The feeling of growth and change
still remains there for me,
even when the dead blooms
are cut back,
and the ground is lain bare.

Barren
a garden can still hold
that feeling of beauty,
mystery,
peace,
oneness
connecting oneself with higher levels
of life and light.

Flowers are the songsters
of Nature
singing with the garden orchestra
a living opus
of life in movement and color.

The flowers of my garden
are always evolving - growing,
budding,
blooming.
Then they release their seeds
and return to earth.

My garden is never dead.
It nurtures the soul seeds
of new life
beneath the sleeping ground.

If I Have Sorrow

If you've spent a lifetime putting your life on hold waiting for the "right" moment, then one day you'll wake up and find that all you have is a bucketful of regrets and sorrows rather than a bucket filled with memories and experiences. Life is meant for living in our present moments not wasted thinking about what we would like to do when we have the time, when we finishing making enough money (whatever "enough" really is), waiting for the kids to finish college, and then their kids. The only thing I know is that if you wait too long, then you'll finally meet Godot ("Death"), and instead of having memories, you'll have sorrows. Sorrow and regret for the adventures you wanted to live, but were too self-afraid or self-absorbed to try.

Remember the first time you jumped off a diving board? You know that you wanted to jump. You saw all the other kids running and jumping off the end, some actually diving head first. You saw how much fun they were having; heard their screams of delight. But that little voice in your head kept on telling you not to try. Deep down inside you knew that it would only take one jump to break the ice, break the chain of fear. One jump and a whole new world of laughter and glee would be yours. You might even have inched-by-inched yourself to the edge and looked down. What actually was only 2 feet or so away now seemed miles and miles away. Some of you slowly reached toward the water, and in a slow motion dance of sorts, eyes closed, made the leap. The dam was broken. Fear was mastered.

You have literally taken the plunge. Running and jumping off the end now becomes an exhilarating experience. You now belonged. No more ridicule from peers; no more lingering doubts about how much fun it would be, because you DID it! You actually did it! Life is full of such opportunities to experience and enjoy.

However, there are those who inch to the edge; look down; and freeze. Fear wins, if only for the moment, that day. They know that it could be done. They see the other kids doing it. But they let personal self-fears stop them. So they slowly turn around and inch back to the security of the hand rails, and feel the personal sorrow of failing to embrace a new experience. It is not failure per se, it is more like limiting your horizons, and it doesn't feel good inside.

Many will try again until they let the desire to jump become stronger than the fear preventing them. Some will never have the courage to take the plunge. It will go into that bucket of regrets. "I'll try it tomorrow" never becomes "today". A life of such moments takes a toll. It limits your horizons; limits your life story.

Do you want to wake up one morning and realize that you have been living a life of regrets? Or do you want to have a life of memories. Have the satisfaction of realizing that at least I've been living my life to its fullest, whether the results were always positive or not.

It's never too late to begin living the life you've dreamed of. Life has enough sorrow and pain as it is without having the sorrow of knowing that you haven't lived at all. Remember life is for the living, for the being in the moment (isn't that why we're called human beings?).

Live the life you desire. And if there are sorrows then let it be for things other than those moments and adventures untried; unlived.

If I Have Sorrow

If I have sorrow,
let it be for things undone,
not for things I have done.

If I have sorrow,
let it be for things un-attempted,
not for things I have tried,
and tried again.

If I have sorrow,
let it be for adventures unlived,
not for those journeys
I had the courage to go on.

If I have sorrow,
let it be for all the todays
that I wasted worrying about
some vague unrealized tomorrow.

If I have sorrow,
let it be for dreams unrealized
because I lacked the courage
to believe in myself.

If I have sorrow,
let it be for love unattained,
not for those loves that I have known,
however briefly.

If I have sorrow,
let it be for time wasted
dwelling on imaginary sorrows of the past.
All were lessons for today.

As long as I have this new day
before me,
let me live in the moment,
follow my dreams,
and not be deterred by the threats
of vague future sorrows.

The Concept of "Beauty"
is Really Simple

You know sometimes the simple isn't so simple; the obvious - not so obvious. Often the beauty of the moment becomes overlooked because we just can't seem to handle the concept of "simple". We can easily understand complex - the ornate, multi-level, ostentatious, even. It is so easy to see that as beauty. But the unassuming beauty of the simple, well that just gets overlooked somehow. Man-made gets attention. God-made taken for granted. A new Mercedes gets the "Oohs" and "Aahs". The beauty of meadow flowers along the roadside, well, it often doesn't even register in our brain.

On some level most of us do realize that beauty, real beauty, is not what is packaged and sold on TV or the social media, but it definitely seems that way at times, doesn't it? It is obvious that so many lives are tainted and manipulated by those who control the media for profitability. There seems to be a constant striving for some pre-ordained level of physical perfection at least to the eyes.

Seeing real beauty, however, is not about following the crowd, blindly accepting what Madison Avenue pushes this week, narrowing our vision to say "thin is beautiful", or that the packaging is more important than the contents. No, seeing beauty means expanding and opening our vision and definition of what our mind and spirit sees as beautiful. When we do so, we begin to live life more fully.

Beauty transcends just the visual to encompass all the senses - touch, taste, smell, etc. There is much truth to the old statement: "Beauty is in the eyes of the beholder". It is even more truthful to state that "Beauty is in the heart of the beholder". Because somewhere deep inside us, on some level, we realize that although that shiny new red sports car is beautiful to look at, it is still only a thing that pales in comparison to the simple beauty of say a dandelion in the hands of a small child.

In fact, if you truly want to know what beauty is, just think as a child. They know right away which of the two, red convertible or dandelion, is more beautiful.

Beauty is Really Simple

Children understand real beauty.
Oh they're attracted to flashing bright lights,
and lots of movement,
but when it comes down to choosing
what is truly beautiful,
they have the perfect eye for it.

Given the choice,
will they choose the sleek Black BMW,
or a clump of dandelions
growing by the curbside?

OK times up!
I think most of us know the answer
to that question.

When you get down to it.
beauty is in
the simple,
the natural,
the real.

There Must Be Dragons Still

You know what got me back into poetry writing? - Dragons. I was thinking how sad and dull the world would be without dragons. You know we Irish poets dwell upon such important questions of existence like that, and we express ourselves through the magic of poetry.

It first started when I had what many would call a "real" job many lay-offs, down-sizing, right-sizing, capsizing ago. I was in one of those management development programs companies like to brag about. As part of our development we had to give a 20 minute presentation on any topic of our own choosing. I was pondering this deep esoteric question at the time - "Are there any more dragons?" So instead of giving a brilliant talk on something like the sex-life of a ping pong ball, surfing, or gun control, I decided to give my presentation on the need to protect these endangered creatures.

So I thought besides opening with a bad joke how could I get my audience's attention. How? How about opening with a stirring poem about dragons? So I did, and for the next 3 years I was known to those who heard my presentation as "the Dragon Master". I still got laid-off 2 months before being vested, but that is how the cookie crumples and cut throat management manages.

Anyway, back to the more important topic of dragons. First off, they are not mindless monsters of wanton destruction as often portrayed by Western Civilization. This is a misconception spread by the Church trying to use dragons as a symbol of evil. Dragons are intelligent beings of great depth as often depicted by Eastern cultures.

Almost every society has a mythology that includes dragons. Carl Jung correctly identified them as archetypes of humanity, a symbol of universal unconsciousness. Carl Sagan speculated that belief in dragons was coded into our DNA going back to the days of dinosaurs. But whether they are part of our evolutionary process or come from the planet Pern, dragons stoke the fires of our imagination. And imagination is one of the fundamental elements making us cognitive beings. It helps us become creators, one with the Infinite. So yes, dragons are that important!

As for me, I cannot imagine a world without dragons. I hope that you feel the same way, too.

There Must be Dragons Still

Looking into azure-tinted skies
on a brisk clear day
brings back faint memories
of when dragons used to play.

When scanning the horizon,
one used to wonder
whether it was clouds or dragon smoke

being carried by the winds.
But now we know it's only puffy clouds
drifting in the breeze,
and not the smoke of a dragon
rising from its lair.

But once in a long, long while
a cloud will cross my view
that has a shape reminiscent
of a dragon,
if only this was true.

Oh! there still must be dragons,
if only I knew where to look.
Because the thought of a world
without their magic
is much too harsh to view.

Oh! There must be dragons…
still.

9-11-01: A Day of Change and Transformation

For most Baby Boomers it is easy to remember where they were for two events: the assassination of JFK and 9-11-2001. JFK was killed when we were young and fill of a rare kind of hope for the future; 9-11 happened in maturity, when there was still some lingering hope that change was still possible.

The images from the collapse of the World Trade Center Towers are a horror that will live forever in our minds. I used to work downtown, and I went in to the Towers quite often. I almost took a job there back in the 1970s. I remember during the interview looking out of the window and seeing a helicopter flying below us over the Hudson River. You could feel the building sway. It was somewhat scary being so high up and the windows seemed to go down to the floor. I took an express elevator to a local one; a vertical subway system. That place was its own mini-city. That job never happened and my life went off in a different direction.

When JFK was shot I was in high school: Archbishop Molloy HS in the Briarwood Section of Queens - the lighted cross that you see from the Van Wyck Expressway when traveling from the JFK airport (Idlewild, in those days) to the city. Everyone openly cried. All dreams of Camelot died.

When 9-11 happened I was working in the commercial aircraft division for a large military-related electronics company. At first we thought that it was an accident involving a small plane, much like what happened to the Empire State Building many decades ago. But when the full horror of what was happening became apparent we were stunned. All work ceased. In fact we were released from work. I went and took my young daughter out of school and tried to take her to the beach to be away from the news and find some peace, but the bridges to the beach were all closed.

I came home and wrote. I wrote for the next several days. I had been working on a poetry project similar to one I had done the year before. I always feel so vibrant and more alive in September, which is one of the best months on Long Island. Work on that project stopped; work on everything else stopped, too. I just started writing, expressing my feelings directly from my heart.

How I wish we could return to those times when we were full of hope. It can happen, but it will require everyone to turn from hatred and embrace love.

A Clearing Sky

The clouds and mist of death
slowly dissipates;
a clear blue-skied day is revealed.
You can hear birds call.
White clouds drift
against the bright azure blueness.

I notice that even the moon
has remained to enjoy the day.
Simple things now so very important.

A tidal wave of hatred
has washed over the land;
The landscape forever changed
in everyone's minds and hearts.

But the shoreline of freedom remains.
The soul of the land is vibrant
and alive;
new life begins.

A moment of silence and reflection
feeds our spirits.
Honor their names;
keep their spirits alive.
The soil of freedom
has been enriched
by their blood.

The fog is almost gone in most areas.
The sunlight of a new day shines.
Hope is reborn amidst rubble.
An eagle flies freely
across the expanse of blue skies.

I'll Drink to That and Did

I'm not quite sure why I've decided to write about this topic even though it is a big part of my life story. I guess I'm writing this because of the weather. It was hot the other day, and today, too; not that unusual for July, so I began thinking wouldn't a nice cold beer taste great just about now. I could say that any day really. It's funny that I still think like this at times, but for me this is normal and probably always will.

It's not that I have a drinking problem. It's more that I had a stopping problem. As the old saying goes - one drink is too many, and a 1,000 isn't enough.

Don't worry this isn't going to be one of those drunk-a-logues. This is more than some rambling on what could-have-been. Bottom line it is not worth my time thinking about any of them. When one spends a good portion of their life in his cups, the mind is already working triple time thinking about what they should be doing; what they could be doing; what they would be doing if they were not spending their time on the bar stool of time lost in doing nothing except self-pitying thinking. I was always going to get around to all these different projects and goals right after the proverbial "one more for the road". But like tomorrow it is always just one drink away.

No lamentations here. It would just be a waste of time, and my time is too valuable to waste anymore. This was more of a random self-observation about ancient history. Of little value to today's living but good stuff for a poem though:

Sitting Here on the Barstool of Time

Yesterdays are forever,
sitting here on the barstool of time.
The portals of time are mine
to pick and choose
which door to enter,
which past events
to relive and re-orchestrate,
to do whatever my feelings
and heart dictates.

I can travel back upstream
on this time ship to yesterdays
to any time I wish
sitting here on the barstool of time.

On my time machine,
the corner bar stool of my ego mind,
I drink my life away
with shooters of misery,
and chasers of self-pity.
"If you don't mind there, bartender,
another round if you please."

My credit is always good
here in my private hell,
the neighborhood tavern of my mind.
The babes are always hot,
mine to pick and choose.

Lost relationships can be renewed;
loves relived;
past hates and pains forgotten
or intensified
depending
on the bent of my thoughts.

Heck, anything is possible
except a real life
sitting here on my personal
barstool of time.

Guess What?
You're just in time for the next round.

Be That Poem

It's April. It's also National Poetry month. It's spring also, although it doesn't really feel like it yet, but it will soon (fingers crossed here). Baseball has returned and the Yankees won their opening game, so there's still order to the universe.

All I know is this. With the emerging flowers comes rebirth. Life is returning. I feel that I need to join with this flowing force of light and energy and get back to my roots - writing. I've hardly written over the winter. This doesn't mean I didn't want to. I just didn't and I've suffered for it.

It's almost like death not being true to who you are. We were born to create. It is what makes us children of God. It is in our acts of creating that we become connected with our Creator.

All I can say is this: Don't let anyone or any situation stop you from being true to your essence. Be what you were meant to be! Most of all don't allow yourself to become your own worst critic. Silence that inner judge; that ghost of some criticizing parent, authority figure or partner; that self-perfectionistic inner voice.

Being who we were meant to be is not about being the best there ever was. It is about being the best that you can be to yourself!

Be that Poem

Some days, it is easier
to be a poem
than to write one.
Easier to flow with the music of life
than capture it with written words,
or well-crafted phrases

On such a day
I must listen to the poetry
created by the flowers,
the poems of clouds in azure blue skies;
The music of a meadow
alive with buzzing life.

On such a day
I need to close my eyes,
and dance in the meadow,
fly in the sky,
sing with the flowers.

On such a day,
I need to drop the pen,
and just be that poem,
not write one.

Does Magic Still Exist?

I know that we are not alone. I know that we are never alone. This is regardless of whether there is life on other planets as we know it, or not. The Universe itself is alive, an organism with a soul. Other worlds, dimensions, wormholes, whatever you choose to call them surround us. Fairies, little people, sprites are among us, maybe on a different dimensional vibration level, but they are here. Most of us are too de-sensitized to feel their presence, which is fine with them, since they aren't too crazy about most of us.

To feel the presence of magic one must still the ego mind and open the senses. To discover many of the wonders of our world one must slow down, stop, quiet the chatter of the mind and just listen. Then just observe, don't judge, don't deny, don't question; just listen and be open. It is at such times that the secret treasures of life become observable. You will then be able to see the magic that surrounds us. In such a state the senses become attuned to their surroundings. It is then that you will begin to notice the traces and glimpses of the little folk; feel the air being moved by fairy wings; see and feel the magic.

Our world needs magic. It needs to believe in mythical creatures. Poets were once the storytellers of this magic; spreading the tales once told by firelight long before the age of cable TV and satellite. You can still listen to these tales though; however, you must quiet your inner self. Your heart and spirit needs to be open, ready for the quiet voice of the poet to begin an epic tale. It can happen. The magic is still here.

Where Mermaids Still Sing

Teach me, dear child,
teach me how to listen
to the mermaids' song.
Where to find fairy charms.
Pick one's special star.
How to sculpture clouds
into magical shapes.

My mind was boundless
at one time.
But life, and the rules;
the need to do the "right" thing;
to keep one's feet
firmly planted in the day,
slowly built walls,
and reduced my world
to one of tunnel vision,
time schedules,
and imposed goals.

Like you, dear child,
I used to play with invisible friends.
None have come

to me in a long, long while.
Would you share your friends with me?

There are worlds
I have not seen;
yet, they exist
right in front of me.
Worlds of birds, flowers
and creepy-crawly things;
elves on butterflies,
and flashes of dragon wings.
It is so easy to see through
a child's open eyes.
Mine have become so clouded.

Please, dear child,
would you take me to where
the mermaids still sing.

Of Course There Are Still Fairies and Leprechauns

In Ireland they still believe in fairies, Sidhe as they are called in Gaelic. Believing in fairies is a common belief in many lands, especially by those who live close to the land and hills and away from the glitter and falseness of big cities. Even those people who believe that Hell is a fabrication of priests to force people to do the right thing believe in fairies. And it stands to reason that fairies should exist. They were definitely here before man.

William Butler Yeats, Ireland's greatest poet, never questioned their existence. He found there was just too much evidence supporting their existence, especially among the people of the countryside, which makes sense since the countryside is the Sidhe's chosen place to dwell, far away from the chaos and negativity of Man. They especially love open fields where you can sometimes catch a quick glimmer among the "bucalauns" (ragweed), which as Yeats pointed out in his *The Celtic Twilight* is sacred to them.

They often dwell in magical castles of light and color that no huge structure of man can approach nor rival. Man endlessly looks for meaning and answers to life. Fairies laugh at such folly. The Sidhe know what they know. Melancholia is not a malady they suffer from, while so many of today's baby boomers seem to. Maybe jealousy is one of the reasons that man strives to destroy their habitats. Jealousy has so many faces. Happiness and contentment has one.

You can't really search for them, but you might come across some when on a whimsey, when your guard is down and your ego mind is at rest. It is then that your senses are aligned with the subtle. In Ireland, in the back roads of our countryside, one might wander down an overgrown pathway or boreen and suddenly find one's self in an unknown land of sorts and come across a earthen embankment, a ring of whitethorn, a "sceach" as it's known to Druids. If you do, disturb it not. It might be a fairy fort.

Come back in the misty evening and you might be within their midst of "the unfading", the Tuatha de Danaans - unfading because unlike Man they do not age.

What does all this rambling mean? It means it's time to bring magic back into my life. Young children have the sight for it, but it is "taught" out of us and we suffer because of it. I think it is time to embrace fantasy again. It's time to take a whimsey; take time to look for the mists; and be open to whispers of the hillside; there might be fairies or leprechauns at play.

Sceachs Still Exist*

Night visiting is very rare these days now.
Sitting here in my chair of life,
I realize that fairies
don't come around much anymore.

The sounds of roaring cars and motorcycles
must damage their sensitive hearing;
It's not the same as the symphony
of thunder and rain.

Most sacred fairy knolls,
Sceachs*,
bushes and forts,
have been replaced
by congested housing, roads,
chemically treated lawns.

How can one hear their whispering,
their quiet lilting chatter,
over the calliope of cable,
150 channel plus satellite TV?
while we sit,
remote in hand,
anesthetized to the secret wonders
around us.

Storytelling is almost gone,
replaced by video games and computers.
Even campfire tales
aren't necessary anymore;
there's TV on in the trailer.

Artificial light holds back
the incoming tide of nightfall.
Quiet darkness is rare,

And the starry wonders of the night sky
go unseen.
The realms of silence
have been invaded by the army of technology.

Sacred names for sacred places
have been mostly forgotten.
Not entirely forgotten,
but rarely spoken,
except in a joking unsure way.
Hey, you don't want to be thought of as strange,
Do you?

Parallel worlds exist,
fairies still dwell among us.
There are so many worlds
that our modernism ignores.
So, they avoid us too;
shunning the artificial light.

How do I know they still exist?
There's a fairy sceach
in a secret corner of the field behind my house;
untouched by me.
Such places must be free
of the taint of human hands.

Sometimes on a night,
when the mists drift in,
a glimmering radiance of emerald light

flickers for a moment
in the gloaming.
It is enough
to renew my faith.

*Sceach – Irish for ring or fairy fort. A circular enclosure surrounded by an earthen embankment on which whitethorn bushes usually grow.

On the Ebb Tide of Life

Summer's here. I love summer, but I am not crazy about the humidity. I don't do humidity well, or is it "good"? Whatever! The concept is conveyed.

I go to the beach often. Living on Long Island and not enjoying the ocean is a big waste of money in my opinion. Why pay all those taxes and not go to Mother Ocean?

After last winter many of the beaches were pretty beat up, especially Robert Moses. I saw the damage that was done by the surging tides and storms, and the effort done to restore them before the traditional summer season. It gave me pause to think about the power of the raging ocean especially at high tide. We are all familiar with that, but then I started to ponder - What about at low tide when the ocean is quieter?

As a baby boomer, whether I like it or not, I realize that I am on the ebb side of the flow of life. It doesn't mean I'm checking out any time soon, but I now accept that my chances of playing for the Yankees are gone.

Although the high tide action of the ocean gets the most attention, there is a period of peace and acceptance associated with low tide. I now have time to accept life; enjoy it more; live it more. I realize that life is far from over. We all need to realize this and savor every moment of life.

And I will...

On the Ebb Tide

The power of the ocean's flow
is felt on the incoming tide.
A building of momentum,
a surge,
explosions,
fire crashing on rocks.

Life is like that.
A surging battle uphill;
attainment;
engulfment;
then a period of peace begins.

The energy of the high water flow
can bring nutriments,
bring destruction,
but it always brings change.

On the ebb,
assessment can be made
as the lower beach is revealed again
to the light.

It is a time of peace,
re-charging,
quietude,

whatever is done, is done.
A realization comes that nothing
is really controllable.

On the ebb tide
no conflicts;
just change;
acceptance and rest
until the next high tide.

Dancing to the Music of Life

I was listening to some oldies the other day, while working at the computer. The tune playing was an updated version of Little Eva's "Locomotion", which gave me pause to remember the original. I remembered practicing dancing to it in the basement when I was growing up in Queens Village. I practiced dancing to a lot of music in the early 60s; playing 45s and 33 1/3s on the old Victrola [Yes, a Victrola, which was an oldie even in those oldie days. But hey it worked.]

So where am I going with all of this? Not really sure, so I'll let my thoughts just ramble along until they decide where they want to go. So Little Eva, the "Locomotion", dancing in the basement, lead me to remembering watching "American Bandstand" at 4 o'clock in living Black and White. Hey, I remember watching every day, first when it was in Philadelphia; then later when it moved to the Coast. Guys in pegged pants, girls with hair-sprayed beehive hair-dos (Marge Simpson would have fit in with this crowd just fine). I thought that they were Oh so cool.

I was a pretty good dancer in those days (still am in my opinion). In fact, I was voted 2nd best dancer in Archbishop Molloy HS (lost out to little Kenny Evers). I always imagined dancing on American Bandstand. In fact years later I did get to dance on a local Dick Clark wanna-be show - the Clay Cole Show (WPIX, Channel 11). Anyway, what does any of this really mean?

Dance and music are part of the good things that we humans do. It's a natural high - a positive in a world of 6 O'clock News disasters. Dancing is great when done with others, but it can just as easily be done alone. We need more dance and music in our lives. It's another form of poetry; another aspect of creation.

Working on the computer can be boring and lonely. But when I add a little music to the mix - the job immediately becomes more fun. And if I am listening to the right mix of tunes I find myself dancing around the kitchen in my socks, and for a while I'm young again. I feel lite; more than that, I am light.

Dancing keeps me young. I hope to always have a 2-step move all the way to that final dance of life.

Get dem Feet a Movin'

When life gets to be too much,
I know what I have to do.
All I need
is to get up out of my chair,
and get my feet a movin'.
Just dance.
Kick dem shoes off,
and move my feet;
my body will soon follow the swaying beat.

The song of life
may be in my head,
love in my heart,
but, if I don't get dem feet a movin',
then all is for naught.
All this life really is anyway,
is a dance.
And if I don't get dem feet a going,
than I'll never feel the rhythm.

Stars twinkling at night,
shine their brightness across the floor,
that excitement, romance,
makes me want to ask someone
to join me on the floor.
And heck, if they don't wanna dance,
then Hell,
I'll just dance out there alone.

Head thrown back,
eyes open wide
under bright stars or shining sun,
I dance with abandonment and glee.
Whether alone or with another,
it don't matter;
as long as I get dem feet a moving
to life's musical beat.

Always K.I.S.S. (Keep It Simple Stupid)

I often wonder why we humans have to complicate the crap out of almost everything we do. Why, when it is easier to go from Point A to Point B in a straight line, do so many of us come up with these Rube Goldberg methods of accomplishing a simple task? I guess we use the government as our model.

We complicate and over-crowd out lives on a daily basis. We don't usually call it "over-crowding", we call it "multi-tasking". When you really analyze it, it really means that you've found a nice way of saying "you're trying to do too much at once". We don't want to realize this, so we say we're multi-tasking.

In the back of our minds we know that this is not a great way to live, but it is often the chosen way in life to just maintain our status quo. This self-imposed life style is stressful and is destroying our immune systems at the very least.

We are dehumanizing our lives by doing this. We end up forcing out time for those very things that make life worthwhile. We often realize this very late in life, but it does not have to be that way. What a gift to one's self to learn to keep it simple earlier in life. But even later, is better than never.

You know that there are simpler ways of doing life. All one needs to do is strip away the extraneous. You really can just go from Point A to Point B. You really can learn to do just one thing at a time. Just remember the old adage: K.I.S.S. - Keep It Simple Stupid!

You'll kiss yourself when you learn this simple skill. You'll love yourself (and others) when you do.

There is a Simple

In a world filled with too many details,
too much noise,
too many distractions,
too many toys,
how does one find a flower
on the hillside?
See the tree within the forest?
See a star in the night sky?

By slowing down the pace of life;
by looking for the simple.

To live a life less complex,
avoid the man-made
for the god-made.
Stop trying to win the race to nowhere;
meander off the pathways more

rather than rush from here to there
following complex logarithms
of society.

Look for the butterflies
not the jets!

If it's All Nothing What Does Matter?

You know, I recently noticed how I've tended over the years to make a big deal about "nothing" I know that I have certainly made much ado about it. Sometimes it feels that I've been living a life in pursuit of "nothing". Whole days seem to be consumed by it – "nothing" that is. I know that many of the seemingly traumatic events in my life in retrospect were really about "nothing". I tell you, at times "nothing" can cover the skies, blocking out the sun – life, love, tranquility, everything. "Nothing" can fill the horizons and beyond.

Sometimes I realize it is really "nothing" that bothers me, but, nevertheless, it still consumes me. At the time I don't realize it is "nothing". I think it is a big "something". It's only later that I realize that all the hubbub was really about "nothing". I tell you, "nothing" can take up a lot of time.

One should never confuse zero (0) with "nothing". These concepts are really totally unrelated, but are often confused. Zero is not "nothing", and 'nothing" metaphysically can be boundless in scope, which is much more than zero. It is a common form of miscommunication to intermix these terms. It's like saying "love" and "sex" are exactly the same thing. They're not.

Now "Zero" is something. It is a cardinal number indicating the absence of any or all units under consideration. In mathematics, it is an element in a set that when added to any other element in the set produces a sum equal/identical to the element to which it was added (ex. 5+0=5). And just see what happens when you multiply with it.

Now "nothing" has no existence unto itself, except what a person tries to give it. Many of us over the years have given great importance to "nothing". Consider this, that in proper English usage "nothing" takes the singular form of the verb even when it is followed by a phrase containing a plural noun or pronoun. (Ex. "Nothing" except your fears stands in your pathway to happiness). Notice that quite often the concept of "nothing" fits rather nicely with the feeling being referenced – "fears". Just think about it.

Why am I thinking about "nothing" right now? I was reading selections from the notebooks of Leonardo da Vinci. He also seemed to ponder about "nothing" a lot. He wrote: "among the great things which are found among us the existence of Nothing is the greatest. This dwells in time, and stretches its limbs into the past and future, and with these takes to itself all works... and possesses nothing of the indivisible present. It does not, however, extend to the essence of anything." "Nothingness has no center, and its boundaries are nothingness"..."

I may not know much, but I do know this - it's time to stop worrying about "nothing". It doesn't really matter, anyway!

What does it Matter?

Deep in the heart of the matter,
lies the source of its anti-matter.
To every thesis there's its anti-thesis;
or is there?

Day into night,
night into day,
which is it?
Does it matter?

The egg or the chicken,
the chicken or the egg.
To tell you the truth,
to me, it just doesn't matter.

What's the matter with kids today
lamented Socrates, or was it Plato?
Is this a new lament,
or one as old as culture?
Again, does it matter?

Well it matters to me,
for I was a child at some time.
Now I'm a child only in
my inner fantasy.

Matter is what this world is made of
to our eyes and touch.
But the scientific truth is

that it is over 99% nothing.
None of this is to be confused with zero though,
zero really is something.
I know - confusing isn't it?

It doesn't matter
if a rock isn't mostly matter;
it can still hurt my head.

Why should that be?
When one remembers,
that we're composed mostly
of space?

When all things are considered
as to where I fit
in the great scheme of things,
I may be mostly made up of non-matter,
but I know I'm not nothing,
and that really does matter.

No Such Things as Endings

So is this the last section? I don't think so. Books have endings. Movies have endings. TV series have endings, even the really good ones. But does life have an ending? I guess in some respects yes, but in the final analysis of it all, life goes on. We go on. Oh yes our form has changed. Our bodies have changed over our life span. We're not that graceful gazelle any more. I know I have a lot more wrinkles than I had some decades ago. In many respects, however, as we age we have grown more beautiful.

It all depends on how we view and approach life. To me I think it is so important to keep a sense of childlike wonderment alive inside ourselves. By doing so we see life as a new adventure every day, instead of viewing each day as a dull repetition of the day before.

If you ever go to an old-age home (and you really should), you see so many sad, scared and lonely faces. Then you see that one face where the eyes are still radiantly bright and alive with a glint of mischief and inner happiness. That person still has the soul of a child. If I have to choose, I definitely know which person would be my life example to follow.

Right now I'm what is called a baby boomer. Most of my body parts function reasonably well. I've lived my life doing the right things for it, and I've lived my life doing bad things to it. But not one thing I did yesterday and all those yesterdays before can be changed. So, as they say, "no use crying over spilled milk (or beer)"; so I try not to. My life time is too valuable for that. There are too many things to see, experience, be a part of. My time today and my days to come is for creating, embracing, loving, enjoying as a child would, not for whining.

The more we change, the more we come back to our beginnings. We either embrace it, or work at denying and rejecting it. Life really doesn't have anything like endings. There are transitions, maybe, but not endings. In the finality of it all we come full circle to join with our origins of creations.

No Such Things as Endings

There is no such thing as endings.
Life, unlike the movies,
does not fade out;
"The End" flashing across the screen,
nor the more exotic "Finis".
There is no listing of credits
scrolling down in front of our eyes.
No Best Boy,
Best Grip,
Gaffer, whatever
No special thanks to the caterers.

No, those things we see as endings,
are really just scene changes -

new beginnings.
We change;
situations change;
life changes,
rather than ends.

Chapters
may be a more appropriate way
of viewing our lives,
but not endings.
Transformations,
growth,
new pathways;
not endings.

I doubt that death is really an ending;
a change of form maybe,
but not an ending.
Our mind's ego sees life's events
as having endings.
Silly mind.